Professor Michael J Benton – dinosaur consultant
Valerie Wilding – educational advisor
Ben Newth – researcher

Scholastic Children's Books,
Euston House, 24 Eversholt Street,
London NW1 1DB, UK

A division of Scholastic Ltd
London ~ New York ~ Toronto ~ Sydney ~ Auckland
Mexico City ~ New Delhi ~ Hong Kong

First published in the UK by Scholastic Ltd, 2003
(as *Now You Know: Stegosaurus – the dinosaur with the spiky spine*)
Published in this edition 2010

Text copyright © Helen Greathead, 2003
Illustrations copyright © Mike Spoor, 2003

ISBN 978 1047 11461 3

All rights reserved
Printed and bound in the UK by CPI Bookmarque, Croydon, Surrey

2 4 6 8 10 9 7 5 3 1

Contents

Introduction

Do you know how to talk dino? It's easier to say dino names in bits:

Steg-oh-sore-us

Say it slowly, then a bit faster. Got it? Great! Now let's find out what Stegosaurus was really like.

Stegosaurus is a bit of a superstar

Lots of people know Stegosaurus. But why is it so famous?

It wasn't the biggest dinosaur ever ... but it wasn't small, either.

Stegosaurus

You

It wasn't the scariest dinosaur ever …
but it could fight if it had to.

Friendly face

Fierce face

It wouldn't ever eat you … but it could
give you some nasty bruises!

A Stegosaurus
did it!

But Stegosaurus looked strange even
for a dinosaur! That's why people find
it so interesting.

And strange things were happening when Stegosaurus lived. The weather on Earth was warm. There was no ice at the North and South Poles. It was wet, too. There was lots of sea and not so much land. And the land was moving!

Once all the land was joined together. But when Stegosaurus was around the land started breaking into huge pieces. Very slowly these pieces became the continents we know today.

The land didn't have flowers ... or grass. But it did have loads of trees and plants ... and dinosaurs.

Giant Apatosaurus (ah-pat-oh-sore-us)
reached up to nibble the treetops. Little
Dryosaurus (dry-oh-sore-us) munched
on the plants underneath. And when
the dinosaurs slept, tiny, furry Dryolestes
(dry-oh-less-teez) crept out to feed –
without getting squashed!

A bird called Archaeopteryx (ark-ee-op-ter-ix) flew through the skies. It had teeth like a dinosaur and claws … on its wings!

Enormous crocodiles swam in the sea. They had flippers like fish!

There were lots of strange creatures around. But Stegosaurus was one of the strangest. Steg had huge, long back legs. But its front legs were only half as long. This made its whole body slope forwards. Stegosaurus had four flat feet, with

12

stubby toes and fat
claws. The claws
were blunt – no
use for fighting!
  Stegosaurus
couldn't run or move
very quickly. It just
plodded slowly along.

13

Stegosaurus was a vegetarian dinosaur. It only ate plants. Veggie dinos usually lived in herds.

Herds were huge. They had to keep moving to find enough food to feed each dinosaur. A dinosaur in a herd ate anything it could.

But Stegosaurus liked to live alone.

Living alone meant that Steg could do what it liked.

Parp!

And *eat* what it liked. Living alone was good for Stegosaurus, because it was fussy about food!

Steg didn't stretch up to the trees to find food, like other vegetarian dinosaurs. Its nose stayed near the ground to sniff out seeds and cones; sweet, green shoots and fat, juicy fruits.

This is a cycad (sigh-cad) plant.

Sharp, spiky leaves

Fat, juicy fruit

That fruit wasn't easy to get at. But
Steg wasn't easily put off.

Stegosaurus had
a hard, lumpy neck.
The sharp leaves
didn't scratch it.

Stegosaurus had a
funny little head.
The head fitted
neatly inside the
cycad plant.

Instead of front teeth it had a horny
beak. The beak was just
right for nipping
off the fruit.
Mmm, tasty!

Behind the beak, Steg did have lots
of teeth. But they didn't look anything
like yours.

Stegosaurus tooth

They were good for cutting leaves.
They were good for mushing fruit. But
Steg's teeth weren't very strong.

They were not good for chewing.

Gulp!   Gulp!

So Stegosaurus swallowed food quickly.
And the food sloshed about in Steg's
tummy for days before coming out of
the other end!

Gurgle   Phht!

Gulp

The strangest thing about Stegosaurus was its spiky back.

Scientists call the spikes "plates". The plates were made of bone and covered with skin.

The largest plate was this big

The smallest was this big

Scientists know why Steg's back legs were long and why its head was small, but after years and years of studying, they still don't know why it had spiky plates on its spine.

Stegosaurus and its spiky spine

Scientists like a good argument. And they've certainly argued a lot about Steg's plates. There are loads of ideas about what they were for.

Some say:

> The plates were used to attack other dinosaurs.

Hmmm, they do look sharp. But imagine having plates on your back. How would you use them to fight? It wouldn't be easy, would it?

Others say:

The plates helped Stegosaurus to protect itself.

Well, that makes sense, because the plates *looked* sharp and dangerous. In fact they were not sharp at all! But they made Stegosaurus seem bigger … and scarier than it really was.

A scientist called Jim Farlow had another idea. He studied fossils of the plates. Fossils are bones and traces of dinosaurs that have turned to rock over millions of years.

He noticed that the plates had grooves on each side.

Grooves   Grooves

Maybe the grooves were for blood vessels? Blood vessels could carry blood from Steg's body through the plates.

Blood vessels carry blood around plates

Blood flows through Steg's body

Now that sounds really strange, doesn't it? But it gave Jim Farlow an amazing idea...

Jim Farlow said:

The plates helped Stegosaurus to warm up and cool down!

This is how they worked. Stegosaurus stood in different positions at different times of day.

Morning:

Steg stands sideways. Plates catch the full heat of the sun

Blood warms up and flows round the body. Stegosaurus warms up

Afternoon:

Hot sun hits the edges of the plates. Blood in plates loses heat

Sides of plates keep out of the sun

Steg keeps cool in scorching sun!

Evening:

Cool wind blows through the plates. Blood cools down

Blood flows round the body. Stegosaurus cools down. It's ready to sleep

There was another reason why blood
in Steg's plates might be really useful.

Stegosaurus lived in flat, open areas of
land called plains. On the plains it could
see a long way. It could spot danger a mile
off. And danger could spot Stegosaurus.

Ceratosaurus (seh-rat-oh-sore-us) was a meat-eater. It had nasty, sharp teeth and claws. It was smaller than Stegosaurus. But stronger.

Here's what might have happened when the two dinosaurs met…

Ceratosaurus sees Stegosaurus. It notices the spiky plates. But it still thinks Stegosaurus looks tasty.

It gets a bit closer. Suddenly, the spiky plates flush fiery red. Wow, Stegosaurus looks fierce!

When Little Dryosaurus hops into the picture, Ceratosaurus chases after it. Forget Stegosaurus, Dryosaurus will be a much easier lunch!

So Stegosaurus was safe. Phew! Sending blood to its plates made Steg *look* really angry – and it didn't have to move a muscle!

But what happened when Steg really did get angry?

Stegosaurus gets very, very angry

Stegosaurus didn't usually do much more than plod around looking for food and eating.

But some things made it very, very angry.

• Another dinosaur trying to attack.

• Another Stegosaurus stealing its water! Water was as important as food to Stegosaurus. Without water any animal will die.

So Stegosaurus had to fight to survive.
But how?

It didn't have sharp teeth or claws.

Its spiky plates only *looked* sharp.

Well, one part of its body was
absolutely deadly …

It was huge. It had spikes.
They were different from the
spiky plates on its back. The tail
spikes really were SHARP. Yikes!

The spikes were nearly as tall as you!

They were hard, but they weren't just made of bone.

They were bone covered with horn, like the antlers on a deer.

Horn is a little bit bendy. It can make a really sharp point, too. So it's doubly deadly!

The tail was bendy, too. Lots of dinosaurs had stiff tails. But Steg's tail could really swish!

When Stegosaurus got angry, it quickly tucked in its head. There were no plates to protect its head. Steg showed off the plates on its neck instead.

Next Stegosaurus turned to the side – and showed off the plates on its spine.

Then it turned right round – and showed off the spikes on its tail.

Its short front
legs shuffled from
side to side.

It looked a bit
like Steg was
dancing!

Its strong back
legs helped to
swish the tail.

Then Stegosaurus attacked ...
backwards!

WHACK!
It knocked knees.

THWACK! It bashed ankles.

CRACK! It jabbed its tail spikes right into its attacker's body!

Stegosaurus didn't care where the tail swished. Wherever it hit was sure to cause damage.

Vegetarian dinosaurs had all sorts of
weapons.

But Steg's tail was more deadly than all
of them. One whack would send most
dinosaurs running.

But Allosaurus
was bigger than
Stegosaurus
and it was really
mean. A hungry
Allosaurus would
come back and
fight again.

Here's what might have happened:

Allosaurus is hurt after the first fight. But it is watching carefully. Second time round, it knows all Steg's moves.

Steg's plates don't protect its head. The tail doesn't protect its tummy.

Allosaurus hides in the trees. It waits. And waits. Stegosaurus doesn't see it. Steg turns to the side.

Allosaurus runs for Steg's tummy, jaws wide open, claws ready.

Steg's tail doesn't get a chance to swish.

Allosaurus was a clever dinosaur.
Stegosaurus wasn't!

Stegosaurus isn't clever

Scientists can work out how clever a
dinosaur was by looking at fossils of its
skull. The soft, squishy bits of the body
rot away when it dies. So you won't
ever find a fossil of a brain. But
scientists can still find an empty
space where the brain used
to be.

Brain space

Stegosaurus was a big dinosaur. But the space for its brain was tiny!

This is how big it *really* was!

Your cat has a bigger brain than Stegosaurus. A baby has a bigger brain than Stegosaurus. YOU have a much bigger brain than Stegosaurus.

Cat's brain

Your brain

So how did Steg live with such a small brain? For a long time, scientists didn't see how it could. Then someone made a discovery.

There was a second space in Steg's skeleton just like the space for its brain. It was much bigger than the first. And nearer to Steg's bottom than its head! They thought Steg had a second brain.

First brain

Second brain

Scientists thought Stegosaurus needed a second brain because it was so big. Now they think that the space near the bottom held nerves that controlled Steg's legs and tail. But it wasn't really a brain.

Stegosaurus didn't do much.

It didn't have to run.

It didn't have to hunt.

It even stood still to defend itself.

One tiny brain is big enough if all you ever do is eat, sleep and plod about!

Chomp!

And besides, Stegosaurus was part of
a group of pea-brained dinosaurs…

The group is called "armoured" dinosaurs. And they did know about one thing. How to protect themselves!

Stegosaurus looked more interesting than the rest of its family. But it wasn't around for long. After Stegosaurus died out, new dinosaurs with better "armour" took its place.

Ankylosaurus (ank-eye-low-sore-us) was one. It was the widest dinosaur EVER!

Ankylosaurus

You

It had bony plates with sharp spikes all
the way from its head to its tail!

Its tail ended in a huge, bony club!
Ouch!

Euoplocephalus (you-op-low-sef-ah-lus) was a bit smaller. It had loads of armour and a tail-club, too. It was so well protected that it even had bony plates over its eyelids!

If anything tried to attack, Euoplocephalus just tucked its legs in and sat down!

Then nothing could get at its soft belly
and its tiny brain was safe inside that
bony skull!

Like Steg it could swish its tail to
defend itself. But it didn't need to very
often. A dinosaur would have to be
desperate – or daft – ever to think about
attacking Euoplocephalus!

Stegosaurus gets famous

Stegosaurus wasn't the only dinosaur with spiky plates on its spine. There were different stegosaurs in different parts of the world.

Tuojiangosaurus (too-oh-yee-ang-oh-sore-us) came from China. It's got a great big name. But its plates were quite neat and small. And it was only a bit taller than your dad.

Your dad

Tuojiangosaurus

Kentrosaurus (ken-troh-sore-us) came from Africa. The plates on its spine looked much sharper than Steg's. And two long spikes stuck out of its shoulders! It looked nasty, but Kentrosaurus was even smaller than Tuojiangosaurus.

Kentrosaurus

Your dad

But Stegosaurus was the first spiked dinosaur ever discovered. And, it was the biggest of the lot!

A dinosaur expert called Othniel Charles Marsh dug up the first Stegosaurus bones in Wyoming, North America, 130 years ago.
One year later he found a complete skeleton, but the bones had shifted out of place. It was difficult to see what this creature was really like.

Marsh kept looking for dinosaur bones. He found loads of new types of dinosaur. Then, after ten years, he found a whole Stegosaurus skeleton, with almost all its bones in place. He got a really good idea of what this dinosaur looked like.

Marsh called it Stegosaurus, which means "roof lizard", because he thought its plates looked like roof tiles!

But the plates weren't joined to the body. They didn't connect with any other bones. They were held in place by the flesh on Steg's back.

Marsh wasn't sure where the spiky plates fitted on the spine:

Did they lie flat on Steg's back?

Was there one row of plates, or two?

Did they flap up and down?

These questions bothered scientists for many years.

Then, about 20 years ago, a skeleton was finally found that had all the plates in place...

At last experts could say for certain that:

The plates stood up on the spine and they didn't flap!

I'm right

But even today, some scientists think the spiky plates stood in one row and others think they stood in two.

In the whole world, only 12 Stegosaurus skeletons have ever been found – and just one baby. So until someone makes a fantastic new discovery, scientists have still got a lot to argue about.

DINONEWS

MAY 2005

STOP PRESS!
STEG SPIKES CAUSE A STIR

Steg's spiky spine is still causing arguments. So now what do scientists think those plates were for? Well, it's a simple idea: they were there to help

Steg find a mate. Lots of veggie dinos were more or less the same shape and size – four stumpy legs, big tum, fat bottom. Steg also had lots of cousins that all looked a bit alike. Finding a mate to help carry on its dino-family was one of the most important things a dinosaur had to do. And as Steg lived alone a mate could be hard to find. But with amazing-looking plates that stuck out on its back, one Steg could spot another one coming a mile off!

STEGOSAURUS ONE: ALLOSAURUS NIL

Scientists have believed for a long time that a Stegosaurus tail was a weapon to avoid. They thought the spikes might even be sharp enough to stab an attacking Allosaurus right through to the bone. Now, Frank Sanders, from the Denver Museum of Natural History, has worked out just how fast that huge tail could swish… But better than that, he can prove how deadly it was. His team has found part of an Allosaurus backbone and it has a hole in it! What made the hole? Well, a Stegosaurus tail spike fits inside it perfectly…

STRONGEST ARMOURED DINOSAUR EVER!

Stegosaurus's family were all a bit strange-looking. Their weird body features were often there to help them defend themselves. Now studies show that one group of armoured dinosaurs was better protected than all the rest. They're called Nodosaurids. And it's a good job they were well protected, because they had nothing at all to fight with!

Scientists say that the plates on a Nodosaurid's very knobbly back were attached by a complicated pattern of super-strong fibres. It was the way the fibres were laid out that made them so strong.

Material that's used today to make bullet-proof vests works in just the same way. Scientists say – if they had been around long enough – Nodosaurids would have been bullet proof too!

THE DINOS THAT DIED OF THIRST

Over 80 years ago, a huge dinosaur grave was discovered in Utah, North America. It's had scientists scratching their heads ever since. The question they asked was: why were so many Allosaurus bones found in one place?

Usually where lots of bones are found, most of them belong to veggie dinosaurs. Veggies often travelled in huge herds, followed by smaller numbers of meat eaters – like Allosaurus – waiting to eat up any sick or dying dinos. In this grave, however, there were more Allosaurus bones than veggie dino bones.

Now Terry Gates, from the University of Utah, thinks he has the answer. He reckons the meat-eating monsters died of thirst! And this is how he thinks it happened:

• Veggie dinosaurs gather round the water hole, chomping on any plants they can find.
• Rain stops falling. They run out of plants and a few dinos die.

• Rotting flesh smells yummy to meat-mad Allosauruses; soon they gather to gobble it up.
• More veggie dinos die.
• The Allosauruses chomp some more.
• They run out of veggie dinos to eat, so they start eating each other!

• But even the Allosauruses can't survive without water and they die too. A slow, nasty death ... leaving behind a fantastic heap of bones that are gradually buried. Millions of years later, scientists dig them up and start puzzling over how these dinos lived.

Di-yes/Di-no quiz

You've read the book, so these puzzles will be eea-sy! Just answer "di-yes" or "di-no" to each of these sentences:

1 Stegosaurus liked to live alone.
Di-yes/Di-no

2 There were crocodiles with flippers around at the same time as Steg.
Di-yes/Di-no

3 The plates on Steg's spine were really sharp and great for attacking its enemies.
Di-yes/Di-no

4 Stegosaurus liked to eat small mammals. Di-yes/Di-no

5 Steg had a beak instead of front teeth.
Di-yes/Di-no

6 Steg scared off its enemies by lifting and lowering its spikes. Di-yes/Di-no

7 Steg attacked its enemies backwards! Di-yes/Di-no

8 Stegosaurus had two brains. Di-yes/Di-no

9 Euoplocephalus had special plates to protect its eyelids. Di-yes/Di-no

10 Kentrosaurus had spikes sticking out of its bottom! Di-yes/Di-no

Answers

1 Di-yes it did. (See pages 14–15)

2 Oh, di-yes there definitely were. (See page 11)

3 Di-no they weren't at all! (See page 24)

4 Di-no it did not! (See page 14)

5 Di-yes it did. (See page 19)

6 Oh di-no, it didn't. (See page 32)

7 Oh, di-yes it did! (See page 41)

8 Di-no, it did'nt. (See page 50)

9 Di-yes, actually, it did! (See page 54)

10 Ouch! Di-no, it didn't. (See page 57)

How well do you know dinos?

Can you match each dino name with a sentence and a picture?

Allosaurus
Stegosaurus
Apatosaurus
Dryosaurus
Archaeopteryx
Euoplocephalus
Ankylosaurus
Tuojiangosaurus

A really wide dino.
It had a tail-club and armour on its eyelids.
Steg's Chinese cousin.
A veggie giant.
It was a diddy veggie dino.
The most famous one with the spiky spine.
It's got claws on its wings.
A clever meat eater.

Answers

Stegosaurus
The most famous one with the spiky spine.

Archaeopteryx
It's got claws on its wings.

Apatosaurus
A veggie giant.

Dryosaurus
It was a diddy veggie dino.

Allosaurus
A clever meat eater.

Ankylosaurus
A really wide dino.

Euoplocephalus
It had a tail-club and armour on its eyelids.

Tuojiangosaurus
Steg's Chinese cousin.

Stegsearch

```
N A N K Y L O S A U R U S
J L S N F P E K T L M S R
E D R S H G M O Z P B U N
N P W E A P O N S J O R A
I W H N S D L E U M N U I
P K A E M X B Y R S Y A R
S R C L K T P A U J P S A
Y N K R T A M Q A U L O T
K H P J L K E H S X A L E
I Z S N I A R B O W T L G
P C R E N T Y K Y R E A E
S T E G O S A U R U S L V
T E E F T A L F D T N E R
```

ALLOSAURUS	**SPIKY SPINE**
ANKYLOSAURUS	STEGOSAURUS
ARMOUR	**TWO BRAINS**
BEAK	VEGETARIAN
BONY PLATES	**WEAPONS**
DRYOSAURUS	WHACK
FLAT FEET	

There are thirteen words, or pairs of words, hidden in this Stegsearch. Look at the list below and see if you can find them all. It's not easy! They might be written up, down, backwards, forwards or diagonally.

ANSWERS

N	A	N	K	Y	L	O	S	A	U	R	U	S
J	L	S	N	F	P	E	K	T	L	M	S	R
E	D	R	S	H	G	M	O	Z	P	B	U	N
N	P	W	E	A	P	O	N	S	J	O	R	A
I	W	H	N	S	D	L	E	U	M	N	U	I
P	K	A	E	M	X	B	Y	R	S	Y	A	R
S	R	C	L	K	T	P	A	U	J	P	S	A
Y	N	K	R	T	A	M	Q	A	U	L	O	T
K	H	P	J	L	K	E	H	S	X	A	L	E
I	Z	S	N	I	A	R	B	O	W	T	L	G
P	C	R	E	N	T	Y	K	Y	R	E	A	E
S	T	E	G	O	S	A	U	R	U	S	L	V
T	E	E	F	T	A	L	F	D	T	N	E	R

Do You Know Dinos?

Index

"These books … provide a great deal of information in a highly accessible way using a small amount of easily read text imaginatively combined with plenty of line drawings … a good choice for dinosaur fans who are also reluctant readers as well as those who are already enthusiastic." *Wordpool News*